Excellence in Leadership

Volume 1

8 Skills for Leaders of All Ages

by
Dr. K. Preston Anderson

authorHOUSE™

1663 LIBERTY DRIVE, SUITE 200
BLOOMINGTON, INDIANA 47403
(800) 839-8640
WWW.AUTHORHOUSE.COM

First published by AuthorHouse 09/27/2005

ISBN: 1-4208-7742-9 (sc)

Library of Congress Control Number: 2005907811

Printed in the United States of America
Bloomington, Indiana

This book is printed on acid-free paper.

Table of Contents

Introduction

Introduction

Among the youth and young adults of today are the future leaders of business, industry, religion, and governmental bodies. These include future Presidents of the United States of America, future Speakers of the House, future Chief Executive Officers of many Fortune 500 companies, future Commissioners of the National Basketball Association, future leaders of religious congregations both large and small, and future leaders of many other organizations. The looming question is where are these young people receiving their leadership training and what kind of training are they receiving?

In a society where youth are often viewed as adhering to the pop culture of the day, there are also many young people excelling well beyond the levels of achievement established by previous generations. There are many youth and young adults who desire to do good and leave a positive mark on the world. A leader of a worldwide organization recently made the following statements about the youth of our day:

- Never before has there been such a generation of youth.
- In so many ways you are remarkable!
- I believe that as a group, you are the finest the world has ever seen. (Hinckley, 2002, pp. 3-4)

This same leader then made the following statement, "You are good. But it is not enough just to be good. You must be good for something. You must contribute good to the world. The world must be a better place for your presence" (p. 8). This book is written then in this spirit – to help youth, young adults, and people of all ages to improve their leadership skills in order to make the world a better place.

I recall the days of my own youth when I was asked to work in positions of leadership. These positions, for me, came through opportunities at school, church, and through my experience in the Boy Scouts of America. In my school, I was selected to be the student council representative in the 4th grade and I worked as editor of my junior high school newspaper and yearbook. I served in various leadership positions in my church youth group that allowed me opportunities to plan dances, activities, youth conference retreats, religious meetings, and many other activities. In Boy Scouts I was in charge of coordinating efforts in earning merit badges, planning meetings, campouts, and activities. Aside from formal positions of leadership, like everyone else, I also took on various leadership roles on sporting teams and among groups of friends.

While I worked hard and was able to fulfill these responsibilities with varying levels of success, I don't recall receiving very much in the way of formal leadership training. I hope this book will help to provide better leadership training for young people through two separate means.

First, leaders of youth can use this book as a guide to formulate specific training seminars or sessions centered around the leadership attributes focused on in each chapter. These leaders of youth could include adult leaders of religious youth groups, advisors to clubs and organizations at schools, coaches of various sporting teams, leaders of scout troops, and many other community groups. Mothers and fathers can also use this book to help their own children develop their leadership skills through quality teaching in the home and modeling effective leadership in their familial duties.

Second, the book has been written in clear language and kept fairly brief to encourage leaders of any age to study the pages on their own. While studying this book, I also hope that, through a process of introspection, readers will establish specific goals in each area of focus and then track their own progress by effectively using the pages provided at the conclusion of each chapter. More will be discussed about goal setting and specifically how to use the goal tracking pages at the end of each section in the first chapter of the book.

This book is written as a self-help book not to be simply read through once in a casual manner, but more so as a step-by-step process to enhance your own leadership skills. While a quick reading to gain a view of the overall concept can be helpful, readers will benefit most by making a detailed study of each chapter and then work to implement the principles taught through effectively using the goal-tracking pages at the end of each chapter. With that as a framework for the purpose of this book, let's get to work developing and enhancing your leadership skills as you strive to "contribute good to the world" around you!

Let's get started!

Chapter 1 – Setting Goals

Chapter 1 – Setting Goals

The reason most people never reach their goals is that they don't define them, or ever seriously consider them as believable or achievable. Winners can tell you where they are going, what they plan to do along the way, and who will be sharing the adventure with them.
– Denis Watley –

It seems that all self-help books and programs have a section on setting goals and this book will be no different in that regard. However, the practical, straight-forward approach of this chapter will hopefully enable those who have struggled with setting and accomplishing goals in the past to find success in this regard in the near future.

Let us start this chapter with a general discussion about the importance of goals, particularly in leadership roles. Accomplishments both great and small are the fulfillment of a goal. Goals include things as simple as learning to tie your own shoe as a child to completing an advanced degree at the collegiate level. While the amount of time to accomplish each of the aforementioned goals is vastly different, they are similar in the sense that the goal presented a challenge to accomplish something they desired to do.

The dictionary defines a goal as the purpose to which an endeavor is directed; an objective. Individuals constantly set all types of goals -- including personal and group goals, short-term and long-range goals. People who set and accomplish goals effectively integrate all of these different types of goals to harmonize with the core values they hold. These individuals establish personal goals that contribute to the group goals and short-term goals that lead to accomplishing a long-term goal.

For example, suppose an individual has established the goal of graduating from college. The number of interim short-term goals necessary to complete in accomplishing this long-term goal are almost innumerable. Some of the short-term goals involved in this example could include graduating from high school, studying to do well on the college entrance exams, saving money to pay for college, and many others. If an individual were to establish a long-term goal of graduating from college and not be aware of the necessary steps to complete along the way, successful completion of the goal would be highly unlikely.

It has been said that an unwritten goal is nothing but a dream. Therefore, the goal-tracking sections at the end of each chapter of this book are designed in such a way as to help you establish the habit of setting and writing down short-term goals with the long-term goals in mind. These goal-tracking sections are arranged to provide a few pages for establishing goals of self-improvement in each of the areas of the following chapters. Each of these goal-tracking sections throughout the book is set-up in such a way as to allow you to write both long-range and short-range goals. Notice that the goal-tracking pages are organized with a spot for a long-range goal at the top of the page and then spaces available underneath each long-range goal to list the short-term goals that will lead to the successful fulfillment of each long-range goal.

When establishing these long-range goals, make sure they are clear, concise, and specific. Many individuals establish a goal simply by stating what it is they want to accomplish; however, this does not constitute a goal. For the purposes of this discussion, goals must have three distinct elements.

First, a goal must be clearly stated. Goals rendered ineffective by being vague could include saying you want to get better grades, improve your financial situation, or be nicer to other people. These goals could be more clearly stated by stating specifically what you really want to accomplish, such as, I want to get at least a 3.5 grade point average this semester, I want to have $1,000 saved by the end of the year, and I will offer more sincere compliments to other people this week.

The second essential element of effective goal setting is keeping goals concise. Often people will write a goal that is so convoluted with tangents to the actual objective that the real goal becomes obscured. A concise goal will detail only one objective – if there are other tangent areas that also need addressing, they either fall into short-term goals underneath the long-term goal or are completely separate long-term goals.

The specificity of a goal mentioned earlier refers to the time-frame that the goal will be accomplished in. Notice the examples offered earlier indicate the better grade point average will be accomplished this semester, the savings will increase by the end of the year, and more sincere compliments will be offered this week. Goals that are created without establishing a time-frame for their completion allow too much opportunity for procrastination. Establishing deadlines for accomplishing long-range goals will help to keep you focused on your goals and also keep your motivation level high.

The key to successfully accomplishing a goal in the established time frame is similarly creating deadlines to fulfill the short-term goals that contribute to achieving the long-term goal. Notice that each of the goal-tracking pages has a space provided on the right-hand side of the page to write a completion deadline for every goal you create. Making use of this aspect of goal setting is absolutely vital to your success.

After you begin working on each of these goals, you may realize your initial time frame was not correctly ascertained – you may find you need either more time or less time to achieve a goal. If this is the case, do not hesitate to change the deadline you have established – but always make sure you have a deadline you are working toward!

Many of the past writings regarding goal setting have indicated that an essential part of accomplishing a goal is to read your goals on a daily basis. I have heard suggestions that you write your goals and post them on a mirror in your bedroom or bathroom so you will see them multiple times each day. While I agree that merely seeing your goals on a daily basis will help you to remember what they are, it will be much more beneficial to actually review the progress you are making on your goals each day.

Therefore, each day, don't just read through the goals written in the goal-tracking sections of this book, actually take the time each day to review, not just the goal as it is written on the page, but the progress you are making toward accomplishing the goals written on the page. An excellent way to evaluate the progress you are making toward your long-term goals is to track the progress you are making on the short-term goals that lead to the fulfillment of the long-term goals.

Aside from evaluating your own progress on your goals each day, your success rate will be increased by making yourself accountable to another person for your progress. A noted leader once said, "When performance is measured, performance improves. When performance is measured and reported, the rate of improvement accelerates" (Monson, 1970, p. 87). In order to accomplish this consistent measurement of your performance, establish a relationship with a trusted friend or family member that you can discuss the goals you have set and regularly report the progress you have made.

A common saying that teaches important principles about achieving goals is the question about how to eat an elephant. Of course, the answer to this age-old question is that the eating an elephant is accomplished one bite at a time. In the same sense, the long-range goals you set in all areas of your life can best be accomplished by breaking them down into smaller, more manageable, short-term goals. These short-term goals then become each small bite of the proverbial elephant as you pursue your long-range goals.

As you write each of your long-term goals on the goal-tracking pages of this book, also record as many short-term goals underneath them to facilitate achieving the long-term goal. Using the previously mentioned example of achieving a higher grade point average as an illustration, I will demonstrate the concept of how short-term goals should directly contribute to accomplishing the long-term goal. If you had raising your grade point average this semester as your long-term goal, some of your short-term goals might include completing all homework assignments on time, taking notes on all in-class lectures, attending after-school tutoring sessions, and so forth. As you are successful in accomplishing each of these short-term goals you will be getting closer to fulfilling the long-term goal of raising your overall grade point average.

Another step that will greatly enhance the likelihood of you achieving the goals you record on the goal-tracking pages and throughout your life is to take action immediately. An old Confucian teaching states that the journey of a thousand miles begins with a single step. With that in mind, each time you set a new goal make sure you take some sort of action that very day to begin accomplishing the goal. This first step may be something small, but it will begin your journey on the road that leads to your success. Supposing your goal is the previously mentioned goal of saving $1,000 by the end of the year, initial steps you could take today could include visiting the bank to open a savings account, taking a portion of the money you presently have in your wallet and depositing it in the bank, contacting an employment agency to find out about current job openings in your area, or reading the classified ad section of the newspaper and circle job announcements for which you could apply. These initial steps must take place sooner or later in the process of accomplishing your goal, so do them today and get started on your way to success!

The examples of goal setting and accomplishing them in this chapter have focused mainly on personal goals of self-improvement. Effectively using these same principles in your various positions of leadership are a key component to successful leadership. You can train others you associate with to follow these same principles of goal setting so they can be more effective in setting personal goals which will in turn help them to more effectively work toward accomplishing goals established by the entire group. The same principles of effective personal goal setting apply to the group goals – the main difference is you must use the other leadership skills discussed in later chapters in order to get the other members of your group to want to accomplish the group goals.

Now take some time to ponder and record your personal goals on the following pages.

Remember – don't just lead... **lead with excellence!**

Setting Goals

Long-Range Goal	Deadline
Short-Range Goals	**Deadline**

People are not lazy. They simply have impotent goals—that is, goals that do not inspire them.
– Tony Robbins –

Setting Goals

Long-Range Goal	Deadline

Short-Range Goals	Deadline

Goals are not only absolutely necessary to motivate us.
They are essential to really keep us alive.
– Robert Schuller –

Setting Goals

Long-Range Goal	Deadline
Short-Range Goals	**Deadline**

If one does not know to which port one is sailing,
no wind is favorable.
– Seneca –

Setting Goals

Long-Range Goal	Deadline

Short-Range Goals	Deadline

Arriving at one goal
is the starting point to another.
– John Dewey –

Chapter 2 – Confidence in Humility

Chapter 2 – Confidence in Humility

Believe in yourself! Have faith in your abilities!
Without a humble but reasonable confidence in your
own powers you cannot be successful or happy.
– Norman Vincent Peale –

At first glance, the terms confidence and humility may appear to be contradictory in their nature. However, good leaders must have both in order to be effective in their leadership roles. As we begin this discussion, it will be necessary to establish a common understanding of these terms.

Confidence is defined as trust or faith in a person or thing; a feeling of assurance, especially self-assurance. We all have confidence in various things. I have always been confident that the sun will rise each morning, that when I drop an object it will fall toward the earth, and that Spring will follow Winter. By developing a high level of self-confidence, you can possess the same assurance in your own abilities to succeed that you have in the rising sun. The opposite of self-confidence is self-doubt – doubting one's own ability to follow through and complete a task which they set a goal to accomplish.

A dictionary defines humility as being marked by modesty in behavior, attitude or spirit; not arrogant or prideful. I have encountered people in my life that have constantly put themselves down and repeatedly voiced their own views of their inadequacies, believing this is a manifestation of humility. This is definitely not humility – this is nothing more than self-degradation! Manifestations of humility include recognizing others' talents, freely offering compliments to other people, and acknowledging your own faults and shortcomings. The acknowledgement of your own faults does not need to be made publicly, but simply a self-recognition of areas of your life where you can seek improvement.

As mentioned earlier, many people view humility and confidence as being opposites, but they actually are quite complimentary to each other. The definition offered for humility included that it was not arrogance. My experience has shown me that many people confuse confidence and arrogance. Arrogance is self-centered conceit, believing that everything and everybody should cater to your every whim. Arrogance is also generally marked by putting other people down. On the other hand, someone who truly possesses a healthy level of self-confidence does not need to try and put others down to help themselves feel better, but rather will seek to lift and build others in all they do.

Years ago as I was discussing this principle with a group of youth, one young man gave a very insightful example of what we are talking about. As he began to grasp the concept that putting others down is not a sign of nor does it increase your own self-confidence.

He said, "I get it. Don't blow someone else's candle out to make your candle burn brighter." As the group analyzed his analogy, we found same wonderful parallels. If each of us were sitting together in a room and had a single candle in front of us, my candle would not burn any brighter by blowing out my neighbor's light – my candle would remain unchanged as a result of the action.

This same group of youth then came up with many other analogies along these same lines. One of them said, "Don't flush someone else's toilet to make yours look fuller." As I have contemplated this analogy over the years, I have come to like it even more as I actually learned more about how a toilet functions! Bear with me for a minute and follow the logic of the analogy. (The included diagram of a toilet shows the basic plumbing and workings of the inside of a toilet.)

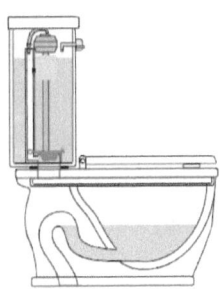 Unless the drain is plugged or a toilet is otherwise not functioning properly, the workings of a toilet will keep the level of the water in the bowl constant. If I were to take and dump a gallon of water into a toilet bowl, exactly one gallon of water would spill over the drain. After dumping the gallon of water into the toilet bowl, I would have the same amount of water in my bowl as when I began – "flushing someone else's toilet" (or putting them down) – does not increase the

amount of water in my own toilet bowl. In fact, as long as the toilet is functioning properly, it is impossible to increase the amount of water in the bowl. The bottom line is that putting other people down is not a sign of confidence – but rather it is a sign of a lack of self-confidence since the person offering the insults is apparently so uncomfortable with themselves that they try to make other people feel bad too.

People who are both confident and humble have the self-assurance necessary to know they are capable of completing whatever task may be placed before them. However, at the same time their humility does not demand that they necessarily be given acknowledgement for their contributions. In fact, a leader with a high level of self-confidence will likely acknowledge the contributions of others on their team before demanding recognition for their own efforts.

An example of a perfect combination of these two attributes is the former point guard for the Utah Jazz, John Stockton. When John Stockton retired in 2003 after 19 years playing for the Utah Jazz, he was the NBA's all-time leader in assists and steals. He directed the offense for the Utah Jazz so effectively that he was able to participate in the post-season playoffs all 19 years that he played professional sports and lead his team to the NBA finals two years. He was selected 11 times for the All-NBA teams, played in 10 All-Star games, won two Olympic gold medals while playing for the United States' Men's Basketball team, and was selected as one of the 50 greatest basketball players of all-time.

With all of these great accomplishments, John Stockton was also one of the most humble players to ever play professional basketball. Unlike many other professional athletes that seem to continually seek the spotlight and attention of the television cameras, after each game, John was more likely to be seen with his wife and children instead of a reporter or sports commentator. The only times that John Stockton would appear before the press was when he was specifically asked by the team's owner – and then only reluctantly would he appear before the press. During these interviews, reporters and sports commentators would want to focus on his record-breaking performance, but he would constantly discuss the contributions of his teammates and their role in the team's success.

Another example of his humility took place the season following his retirement when he was asked to return to the Delta Center in Salt Lake City, Utah, to ceremoniously retire his jersey and number. While other celebrities thrive on that type of honor and an opportunity for one final time in the spotlight, John Stockton asked the owner of the Utah Jazz if he had to actually be there. When he was told it would be nice to have him there, John then asked if he could have his children pull the rope that would unveil the jersey. Once again, when offered the limelight for his many accomplishments, he deferred the honor and credit to those who supported him and helped him achieve these great accomplishments. The sheer magnitude of his accomplishments speaks volumes about his confidence, but the way he carried himself and constantly gave credit to other people proclaims loudly of his personal humility.

Now, take some time to ponder and then write down goals in both the areas of increasing your confidence and developing your humility. These goals should be clear, concise, and specific, and should also have as many short-term goals as necessary to facilitate achieving each of the long-range goals. Remember also to review your progress on these goals daily and report your progress to a trusted friend or family member.

*Remember – don't just lead... **lead with excellence!***

Confidence in Humility

Long-Range Goal	Deadline

Short-Range Goals	Deadline

Always hold your head up,
but be careful to keep your nose at a friendly level.
– Max L. Forman –

Confidence in Humility

Long-Range Goal	Deadline

Short-Range Goals	Deadline

True merit is like a river,
the deeper it is, the less noise it makes.
– Edward Frederick Halifax –

Confidence in Humility

Long-Range Goal	Deadline

Short-Range Goals	Deadline

It is always the secure who are humble.
– Gilbert Keith Chesterton –

Confidence in Humility

Long-Range Goal	Deadline

Short-Range Goals	Deadline

You shouldn't gloat about anything you've done; you ought to keep going and find something better to do.

– David Packard –

Chapter 3 – Prioritize

Chapter 3 – Prioritize

*Set priorities for your goals. A major part of successful
living lies in the ability to put first things first. Indeed,
the reason most major goals are not achieved is that
we spend our time doing second things first.*
– Robert J. McKain –

An important part of succeeding in any endeavor is
the ability to prioritize the work you perform. At any
given moment in time, there are so many good things
we could be doing with our time that we can never
do them all. However, if we don't take the time to
prioritize the work we are going to perform, we might
not accomplish anything!

The word prioritize means to arrange or deal
with in order of importance. To accomplish any long-
term personal goal or motivate and lead others to
fulfill a task requires that adequate thought be given
to prioritizing the work to be done. To describe the
process of prioritizing in a very simple manner would
be to create a list of all of the steps you would like
to complete in accomplishing a given task. You would
then need to categorize those steps into at least three
categories: *Primary Necessity, Secondary Necessity,
and Nice – but not Necessary.*

Every task to be undertaken has these same three
categories of tasks. As an example, let's say you want
to build a house. There are aspects of this process that

fall into each of the three categories mentioned. Items that would be *Primary Necessities* could include things like finding a piece of land to build on and hiring a licensed contractor and architect. Tasks considered to be *Secondary Necessities* could include what color you will paint the walls in the house – it is something you must decide at some point in the process, but you could start the building process first. Items that would be considered *Nice – but not Necessary* in building a house might include finding a corner-lot to build on, crown moldings, hardwood floors, and an indoor bowling alley! These things could certainly turn your home building project into your dream house, but you could also live very well without them.

Now this chapter is obviously not about building a house, remember to look beyond the examples given for the real principles that will guide you in effectively prioritizing the goals in your own life. Let me illustrate the principles of prioritizing with the following example.

While attending a seminar that included a portion on prioritizing, I saw a demonstration that made a good point. However, as I considered further about the implications of the demonstration, I found there was another valuable lesson to be learned other than what the presenter stated. I will describe the demonstration and then elaborate with both of the lessons learned from the demonstration.

As part of his talk, the speaker produced a large glass jar, a dozen apples, a container of dried kidney beans, and a container of sugar. He invited a participant to come to the front and asked them to get as many of the things in the jar as possible. The individual who went to the front, picked up the container of sugar first and dumped the entire thing into the jar. She then poured all of the dried kidney beans into the jar. Finally, she picked up the apples and tried to put them in the jar, but couldn't get any of the apples inside the jar, because it was already full of the sugar and the beans.

The speaker then instructed everyone to assume that the space inside the jar represented the time each of us has to accomplish any given task, the apples represented the really important things in our lives – our highest priorities, the kidney beans represented secondary priorities, and the sugar represented those things that are nice in life – but not necessarily vital. The point he tried to teach was that if we don't take care of the important things in life first, we might not have time to accomplish all of the things that need to be done.

This lecturer then produced a second jar, another dozen apples, a container of kidney beans, and a container of sugar. In an effort to illustrate his point, his placed all of the apples inside the jar and they came right near the top of the jar. He then pointed out that while the jar looked full and that all of the "time" to complete the task was past, he then poured the dried kidney beans in, shook the jar a little, and got many of them into the jar. After doing this, the jar again looked quite full. However, he then began to pour the sugar into the jar, repeatedly shook the jar and was able to pour quite a bit of the sugar into the jar. His point was well illustrated that if we will take care of the most important things first, we can then find time for some of the non-essential things in our life too.

As I later contemplated this demonstration, I came to realize another lesson from the same example. As we each go about our lives doing those things that we each need to do in order to be successful, there are always little pockets of time that we could use more effectively. Just as this demonstration showed how we could fill in the gaps between the apples with other things, we can also find little things to do with some of the pockets of time we have each day. Some of these pockets of time might include while you are waiting for the bus, while you are waiting for your fingernail polish to dry, while you are waiting for a friend to get ready, etc. In light of the previously cited demonstration, my wife calls these periods of time "sugar time".

Let me illustrate this point with an example from my own life. At the age of 19, I made the decision to leave home for two years and work as a missionary for my Church. I was assigned to work in the island of Taiwan. When I received my assignment, I knew nothing about Taiwan or the Chinese language that they speak there. However, I did receive about two months of language training in the United States before leaving for Taiwan.

During these two months, I lived with others embarking in the same service and we did everything together. Aside from eating three meals a day in the cafeteria, our daily routine consisted of about 10 hours of instruction in a small classroom. One of the rules of the training center is that we must always be with our partner or companion.

During my first week at the training center, I found myself very frustrated at all of the time I spent waiting. Since there were over 4,000 people at this same training center, I waited in lines at the cafeteria, I waited while doing my laundry, I waited for class to start, I waited for my companion to finish getting dressed, and so forth. It seems that all I ever did was wait either for someone to get ready or for something to start.

At the end of that first week, I knew if I didn't find someway to alleviate my own frustration with all of the waiting, that I would go crazy before my two months were finished. So I decided that anytime I felt frustration setting in because I was waiting, I would instead pull out a book and read. It was very easy to make sure I always had a book with me. So, during the remaining eight weeks, I was able to start and finish seven books that really helped me in my missionary efforts. These books ranged in size from about 100 pages to over 300 pages in length. All of this reading and learning took place during my "sugar time" – time that I didn't have anything else to do. I continued this same practice during the two years that I was in Taiwan and was able to read many, many more books during this time. I have continued to utilize this same practice in my life by downloading various books and magazines to my handheld computer and then I can read whenever I have a spare minute – regardless of where I may be at the time!

Using time wisely is only one aspect of effective prioritizing. When you are functioning in leadership roles, you must be able to effectively prioritize the use of all of your resources. For example, if you are the head of a student council at school, you are probably given an annual budget for the school year. If you plan big budget parties for back-to-school and Halloween, are you going to have enough money left in the budget for a celebration at the end of the school year?

You might have other constraints placed upon you that require you to prioritize. Continuing with the example of a student council, perhaps your faculty advisor or administrators may limit the number of assemblies they allow you to have in a semester. If you plan and carry out your allotted number of assemblies at the beginning of the year, what are you going to do when the baseball team wins the state championship, but you don't have anymore assemblies available?

You can see that part of prioritizing is looking to the future and sometimes planning for things that you may not be able to completely control. When you are faced with the challenge of prioritizing in a group setting, make sure you get the input of other group members to insure that the priorities you establish are truly the priorities for the whole group and not just your own desires.

Counseling with those around you is another key component of effective leadership. Effective leaders will listen to the input of those whom they lead, because many times other people can see aspects of a problem that you may not see because you are too closely associated to the problem.

As this chapter comes to a close, take some time to reflect on times in your own life when you have effectively prioritized your efforts and perhaps some times when you could have improved. Then record some goals for how you can improve this aspect of your leadership skills. Make sure you set some goals that are personal in nature and also some that reflect the current leadership roles you occupy. By setting goals in multiple facets of your life, you will enjoy the benefits of living a well-rounded and balanced life.

*Remember – don't just lead... **lead with excellence!***

Prioritize

Long-Range Goal	Deadline
Short-Range Goals	**Deadline**

Set priorities for your goals. A major part of successful living lies in the ability to put first things first.
– Robert J. McKain –

Prioritize

Long-Range Goal	Deadline

Short-Range Goals	Deadline

Most people fail in life because they major in minor things.
– Tony Robbins –

Prioritize

Long-Range Goal	Deadline

Short-Range Goals	Deadline

Decide what you want, decide what you are willing to exchange for it. Establish your priorities and go to work.
– H. L. Hunt –

Prioritize

Long-Range Goal	Deadline

Short-Range Goals	Deadline

The key is not to prioritize what's on your schedule
but to schedule your priorities.
– Stephen R. Covey –

Chapter 4 – Delegation

Chapter 4 – Delegation

You can delegate authority, but not responsibility.
– Stephen W. Comiskey –

Another vital skill for successful leadership is the art of delegation. Leaders who excel in their roles do so because they first realize they cannot accomplish everything by themselves and, second, they involve other people to accomplish difficult tasks.

Delegation is defined as the act of committing or entrusting something to another. Aside from merely allowing other people to contribute in the fulfilling of a goal or project, delegation is essential to successful leadership for many other reasons.

One advantage of delegation is that as more people have an assignment in conjunction with an activity, not only do they feel more important as a result of the responsibility, but you have automatically increased the attendance at the activity. For example, you could plan an activity and bring all of the refreshments yourself, but you have not given anyone else a reason to attend the activity. Look for the principles of delegation as we take this example further.

Let's suppose that you are having various kinds of snack foods at a party – this might include chips and dip, soda pop, a vegetable tray, and mini-éclairs. Instead of bringing it all yourself, assign three people to bring two bags of chips each, another two people to bring dip, four people to bring a 2-liter of soda pop each, divide the vegetable tray around to six different people, and finally two people to bring the mini-éclairs. By simply using the skill of delegation you have increased the guaranteed attendance at the party from one (just yourself) to 18 people – plus as a result of having more people attending the party, you will also have more people mentioning the party to their friends also.

An important thing to remember with delegation, though, is that after you have given somebody that responsibility, you have to let them have 100% of that responsibility. As the leader, the one who gave the assignments, you must be willing to completely let go of those assignments and let the other people succeed or fail on their own. I have seen leaders in the past who have difficulty completely letting go after delegating assignments in two specific ways.

The first way many leaders have difficulty in letting go of an assignment is allowing others to use their own judgment in how to carry out their duty. Continuing with the example of refreshments for a party, when you assign someone to bring a bag of chips, you must be satisfied with whatever kind of chips they decide to bring. On the other hand, if you need to have the job done a specific way – for example, you must have tortilla chips instead of potato chips – you need to make that clear when handing out the assignments. However, once the assignment has been given, you must allow people to use their own agency and creativity in fulfilling the assignments they have been given.

The second way in which many leaders have difficulty letting go after delegating responsibilities is by not allowing other people to fail. I have seen too many leaders always have their own back-up plan ready in case somebody does not follow through with their assignment. Few things could be more detrimental to another person than to remove the natural consequences for the choices they make. By always having your back-up plan ready to go, the only thing you teach your followers is that if they are going to "drop the ball", somebody else will be there to keep it from hitting the ground. This gives people a false reassurance, because in "real life" there isn't always somebody there to prevent failure from occurring.

Imagine if someone in the previous example did forget their assignment for the refreshment table, what is the worse thing that could happen? The worse thing arising from such a scenario is that there may be a few less chips to be eaten at the party. However, the lesson that individual would learn about responsibility would be more valuable than any inconvenience suffered by the rest of the guests.

A simple way to insure that people are going to follow through on the assignments they have been delegated is to establish a pattern of reporting on their progress. Let's consider this principle while continuing with the same example of planning a party. If food assignments are delegated at one of the first meetings of the group, have each person report on their progress at subsequent meetings. Not only does this serve as a natural reminder for each person, but it also allows a time for clarification if a previous misunderstanding occurred.

Another consideration when delegating responsibilities is the abilities of those involved. Let me use another personal example to illustrate this point. My wife and I have three beautiful girls and my wife does a marvelous job of having their hair fixed every morning before they go to school. As a husband and father, I try to do my part around the house to keep things operating smoothly. However, we have learned that my abilities in fixing hair – braiding, making pony tails, etc. – are quite inferior to my wife's abilities. Assume for a minute that we have a family outing on a Saturday morning and we are in kind of a hurry to get on our way. Rather than try to help and fix the girls' hair, I will tell my wife to let me worry about fixing breakfast or cleaning the dishes and have her focus solely on fixing hair. In this way, she is doing the task she is most qualified for and I am fulfilling a task that I can adequately do. This is an important principle to remember when delegating assignments to members of the group.

When working with various groups and delegating assignments, often times financial considerations can be important factors to consider. Perhaps some of the people in your group cannot afford to buy anything to bring to the party for refreshments, but they still want to be involved. With almost any activity, there are plenty of opportunities to help that do not require the spending of any money. If you are having a party, somebody needs to be responsible to set-up the tables and chairs, monitor the refreshment table during the party to make sure the food is not running out, and, of course, there is also plenty of work to be done in cleaning up. Make sure you give everybody an opportunity to participate in the activity in some manner.

Along with considering an individual's abilities when delegating assignments, an effective leader will also think about somebody's need for further growth and development. While I definitely have a need for further growth in the area of fixing my daughters' hair, the best time to experience that growth is not when we are rushing to get out the door! However, try to find opportunities that will stretch people's abilities and lead them to new levels of achievement.

My father once told me that sometimes it wasn't as important to get the best man for the job as it is to get the best job for the man. I don't know if I fully understood what he meant when I was a younger, but I think I have come to a greater understanding over the years. I think everybody has attended various functions and noticed something that wasn't done the same way they would have done it. You may have thought you could have done a better job than those carrying out the assignments and, at times, you might have been right. However, often the personal growth that individuals receive from completing a task is more important at that time than having the task done in the most perfect manner.

So, when delegating responsibilities throughout your group, also consider who could use the opportunity to grow and which assignment would help each individual to grow in the way they need most at that time. Seek to find a balance between finding a task that will give them opportunity for personal growth without giving them more than they can handle and causing unnecessary frustration.

A specific way that the art of delegation can help to bless the lives of other people is in working with people who have physical handicaps or other special needs. Despite their limitations, these people are always wanting to assist and help other people and feel that they have made a significant contribution to the success of the group or activity. Individuals with special needs can often be involved in carrying out assignments through assigning them to work in a team with another member of your group. Perhaps you could assign an individual with special needs to help two other group members set-up chairs for the party. Do not let someone's special needs deter you from involving them in the activity – more often than not they are very capable of completing certain tasks as well as anyone else and they always enjoy a great feeling of satisfaction and accomplishment for helping the group achieve a goal.

Now, take some time to ponder on the artful skill of delegation and discover ways you can improve this in your own life. Then write down these goals on the following pages in a clear, concise, and specific manner. Don't forget to keep track of your progress in this and the other areas you have set goals in the goal-tracking sections of this book.

*Remember – don't just lead... **lead with excellence!***

Delegation

Long-Range Goal	Deadline

Short-Range Goals	Deadline

Surround yourself with the best people you can find,
delegate authority, and don't interfere.
– Ronald Reagan –

Delegation

Long-Range Goal	Deadline

Short-Range Goals	Deadline

Delegating work works,
provided the one delegating works, too.
– Robert Half –

Delegation

Long-Range Goal	Deadline
Short-Range Goals	**Deadline**

Don't tell people how to do things, tell them what to do and let them surprise you with their results.
– George S. Patton –

Delegation

Long-Range Goal	Deadline

Short-Range Goals	Deadline

The best executive is the one who has sense enough to pick good men to do what he wants done, and self-restraint to keep from meddling...while they do it.

– Theodore Roosevelt –

Chapter 5 – Servant Leadership

Chapter 5 – Servant Leadership

The service we render to others is really the rent we pay for our room on this earth. It is obvious that man is himself a traveler; that the purpose of this world is not "to have and to hold" but "to give and serve." There can be no other meaning.
– Sir Wilfred T. Grenfell –

Sometimes people who are placed in positions of leadership have the mistaken idea that they are somehow "above" those they are leading. Some leaders believe that the people they are leading work for them – however, leaders who work most effectively take the opposite view. These leaders understand that they fill the role of working for and serving those that they are leading.

A few years ago I became acquainted with a theory of leadership known as *Servant Leadership.* This theory of leadership encourages the leader to seek opportunities to serve those whom he or she is responsible to lead. Literally volumes of books and articles have been written about this style of leadership. I will summarize the main point of this style of leadership in this chapter and provide examples to illustrate this theory of leadership in action. (If you would like to learn more about the theory of *Servant Leadership,* you can find many books at your local library or bookstore, or you can also find a lot of information at on the Internet, specifically at www.greenleaf.org.)

One of the foundational teachings behind *Servant Leadership* comes from the New Testament. While this teaching does come from the Bible, it is important to note that this style of leadership is not only applicable to followers of one certain religion. Experts in the field of *Servant Leadership* have also pointed to great examples of this style of leadership among the ancient Chinese philosophers, modern African leaders, and many other political and corporate leaders.

The foundational New Testament teaching behind *Servant Leadership* is recorded in St. Matthew 20:25-27. At this time, Jesus was trying to teach his apostles about the importance of service in leadership. He said to them, "Ye know that the princes of the Gentiles exercise domination over them, and they that are great exercise authority upon them. But it shall not be so among you: but whosoever will be great among you, let him be your minister; and whosoever will be chief among you, let him be your servant".

I want to emphasize again that this style of leadership is not limited to followers of one specific religion. The theory of *Servant Leadership* entails many different aspects and attributes. However, for the purposes of this section of the book, we will only focus on the general principle that leaders out to seek to serve those whom they lead.

A natural outgrowth of this style of leadership is that your followers will be more dedicated to fulfilling their own roles in seeking the common goal of the group. During my years working as a teacher, I have had numerous principals that have been the appointed leader of the faculties which I worked on. Of all these principals, one sticks out in my mind as exemplifying this principle of servant leadership.

Shortly after joining this faculty, I remember this principal came into my office one morning near the beginning of the school year and asked me what he could do to make my job easier that day. I replied that I thought I had things under control and I couldn't think of any help that I needed at that time.

He came into my office again the next day and we had a similar conversation. On the third day, after having the same conversation again, he informed me that I needed have something for him to do the next day when he came to visit my office. Following his request, I did have something for him to do the next day. I believe I gave him a handout I was going to use in class that day and had him make copies for my students.

When he returned the copies to my office, he explained to me that his main job as the principal was to make my teaching job easier. So, he would always be looking for something to do each day to help each member of the faculty. I worked for this man for five years and he stayed true to his word. He always looked for opportunities to serve those he worked with, whether at work or away from the job.

His attitude of service let me know that he really was concerned about me as a person and wanted me to be successful. My natural response to this kind of attitude was to care about him in return and try to help him in anyway possible. It was a wonderful five years as we would constantly look for ways to help each other to be more successful in our personal and group goals.

I think most people can remember influential leaders they have worked with in the past. As you consider the leaders you have worked with in the past, think about the service they either did or did not offer you in helping to complete projects and accomplish goals. Did the amount of service they offered affect what you thought of them as a leader and how loyal you were to them or how committed you were to the goals of the group?

The service you offer to those you lead does not have to be extraordinarily large acts of service. In fact, the subtle acts of service sometimes become more meaningful than something that was carefully planned and carried out. An exceptional, yet often overlooked, form of service is to offer encouragement and public praise for the good things that other people do. As you offer these public accolades for a job well done, others in the group will naturally renew their commitment and desire to make positive contributions to the group efforts.

As I searched for an example of a well-known person whose life could illustrate the idea of rendering service in leadership, I thought perhaps none would serve a better example than Diana, Princess of Wales. Princess Diana was different than many members of the royal family because she did not rule from a palace, but rather mingled with everyone and used her position of leadership to promote good throughout the world.

During her life, Princess Diana could constantly be seen at orphanages and hospitals, visiting people who were suffering from illness or tragedy. When the news cameras would show Princess Diana in these settings, her sincerity was clearly manifest. It was obvious to people around the globe that her motivation was not just to be seen in the public eye, but she was clearly prompted to embrace these causes out of genuine concern and love for others.

Through rendering this selfless service, Princess Diana's legacy and her work did not come to an end with her unfortunate death in 1997. By offering service and embracing causes in life, others throughout the world continue to support the work that Princess Diana supported. Over 350 organizations benefit from contributions made to the Princess Diana Foundation even following her untimely death.

Whenever I think of service, I always reflect on a poem that I memorized as a young man. That poem goes like this –

Suppose today was your last day on earth,
The last mile of the journey you trod.
After all of your struggles, how much are you worth?
How much can you take home to God?
Don't count possessions, your silver and gold,
For tomorrow you leave those behind.
All that is yours to have and to hold,
Is the service you render mankind.

      – Author Unknown –

As you work in various positions of leadership, remember that the best way to secure the loyalty and support of those you lead is for them to truly feel your love and concern – and there is no better way to show this than through sincere service.

Another brief example of a leader providing selfless service occurred during the playoffs at the conclusion of the 2003-2004 basketball season. At a playoff game between the Portland Trailblazers and the Dallas Mavericks, a 13-year old girl, Natalie Gilbert, was selected to sing the National Anthem prior to the opening tip-off. Despite singing the song perfectly numerous times before this event, she forgot the words part way through the song. As this brave young lady stood there obviously nervous and scared, the head coach for the Portland Trailblazers at that time, Maurice Cheeks, stepped to her side and sang along with her for the balance of the song. After a couple more lines of the anthem had been sung, Coach Cheeks encouraged the crowd to join in the singing.

Following this event, rather than accepting the accolades of the fans and the press, Coach Cheeks continually complimented Natalie for her courage. Not only did the crowd follow Coach Cheeks' example and join in the singing, but people have been praising this move by Coach Cheeks ever since. On the NBA website, literally hundreds of fans have submitted emails praising the humble, selfless move made by this head coach. In one of the emails a fan wrote, "I know his action will be a model for would-be leaders for decades to come." Another email from a fan stated, "We need more men like Coach Cheeks; those who are not afraid to step out of their comfort zones to help another. In this act of selflessness, he taught more to children and adults than he could have ever dreamed of." This example provides another example of a high profile leader offering a small act of service that touched thousands of people throughout the country and the world.

Now, as with the other chapters, take a moment and ponder what improvements you need to make in your own life regarding serving those you lead. After you have given this some thought, write down your goals in the pages that follow. Make sure you include the steps you are going to take to accomplish your long-term goals with specific short-term goals.

Remember – don't just lead... **lead with excellence!**

Servant Leadership

Long-Range Goal	Deadline
Short-Range Goals	**Deadline**

Service is the rent we pay to be living.
It is the very purpose of life and not something you do in
your spare time.
– Marian Wright Edelman –

Servant Leadership

Long-Range Goal	Deadline

Short-Range Goals	Deadline

You don't have to have a college degree to serve. You don't have to make your subject and verb agree to serve. You only need a heart full of grace. A soul generated by love.

– Martin Luther King, Jr. –

Servant Leadership

Long-Range Goal	Deadline
Short-Range Goals	**Deadline**

It is one of the most beautiful compensations of life, that no man can sincerely try to help another without helping himself.

– Ralph Waldo Emerson –

Servant Leadership

Long-Range Goal	Deadline

Short-Range Goals	Deadline

There is no greater calling than to serve your fellow men. There is no greater contribution than to help the weak. There is no greater satisfaction than to have done it well.

– Walter Reuther –

Chapter 6 – Power of Example

Chapter 6 – Power of Example

Example is not the main thing in influencing others. It is the only thing.
– Albert Schweitzer –

The importance and power of your example cannot be overstated in your leadership roles. The standard of example that a leader of any group establishes through the way he or she lives their life will have a major impact on everybody in the organization. The choices you make, both in your personal life and in your role as a leader, will create the atmosphere that will guide everyone in the group which you lead.

The most important aspect of your example is that others will analyze your actions and ascertain whether they are in harmony with the behaviors you encourage others to implement. To put this in modern language, others are watching you to not only see if you can "talk the talk" but if you can then "walk the walk". If, as a leader, you verbally encourage your followers to practice the art of the aforementioned *Servant Leadership*, but they never receive any service from you or witness you rendering service to others, your followers will probably give less credibility to the words you speak.

In the few years following the turn of the millennium, there were plenty of examples of high-profile leaders who did not live their lives according to what they taught. The executives at Enron, WorldComm, and ImClone, illustrate the impact of leaders who set a bad example. People who worked for these companies and the public who invested in them believed they could trust those in the highest ranks of leadership. However, their secret actions were eventually made public and in addition to being imprisoned and facing other disciplinary actions, they face the daunting task of trying to regain the trust of those affected by their poor decisions.

Conversely, let us focus on a truly remarkable illustration of how a leader's positive example and willingness to do what he asked others to do resulted in remarkable results. After the 2002 Winter Olympic Games had been awarded to Salt Lake City, it was discovered that some of the leaders of the bid committee had bribed members of the International Olympic Committee. Following the resignation of these top officials, Mitt Romney was hired as the new Chief Executive Officer of the Olympic Committee. Mitt Romney had made a career previous to this in acquiring companies experiencing financial difficulties and turning them into profitable businesses again.

The challenges Mitt Romney faced were not limited to the controversy surrounding the previous leaders of the Olympic committee. When he took over the planning and carrying out of the Salt Lake Olympic Games, it looked as if the games would be way over budget. Despite these challenges, Mitt Romney was able to turn the Salt Lake Olympic Games into one of the most successful games of modern times – and he did it within his established budget and even returned a profit to Salt Lake City and the state of Utah.

The way Mitt Romney accomplished such a formidable task was largely due to the example he established for others to follow. In order for the Olympic Games to stay within their budget, Mitt Romney called upon the citizens of Utah to volunteer their time and efforts to bring about a successful Olympic Games. However, Mitt did not just call upon others to volunteer, one of his first official acts was to return his entire salary to the Olympic Committee. Mitt Romney then worked on the Olympic Games for the next three years as an Olympic volunteer. Following Mitt Romney's example, more than 32,000 other people volunteered their services to contribute to a successful staging of the Olympic Games.

If we now contrast the current situation of the leaders mentioned in the bad examples with Mitt Romney, the differences are astounding. While the executives of Enron, Worldcom, and ImClone are currently serving time in prison, Mitt Romney is currently serving his first term as Governor of Massachusetts and has been named by many political experts as a front-runner for the 2008 republican presidential nomination.

The type of moral behavior exemplified by Mitt Romney prompted everyone around him to emulate the same high standards of behavior and contribute to carrying out a very successful Olympic Games. In a similar way, if you want those who you lead to work hard and put forth their best efforts, you must first establish this as what is expected by first working hard yourself. Moral behavior is not the only thing that is best conveyed to your followers through your example, but your example will be a powerful tool in many aspects. For instance, as you work to improve your own life in the area of *Servant Leadership*, others around you most likely will see a positive example and feel a desire within themselves to similarly seek for opportunities to serve other people.

The importance of the example you set will be constantly measured against the values you claim to believe in. When your followers see that your words and your actions are in alignment, they will begin to believe the sincerity of your words when you are speaking. Conversely, if your actions do not align with the values you claim to believe, your spoken word will then become hollow and lack the credibility necessary for truly effective leadership.

As you begin to consider possible goals you may set in the goal-tracking section of this chapter, I would like to offer a few suggestions of possible goals. The reason for making these recommendations is that the possibility of goals in this realm are potentially endless. These suggestions will hopefully help your mind to begin formulating goals that will be most meaningful to yourself.

For our first example, let us consider the attribute of punctuality. Assume for a minute that you tell those in your group that you find it extremely important to start meetings on time and, therefore, you expect each of them to arrive on time – or early. How seriously will the members of your group take this request if you are late to the group's meetings or other functions.

If you really want to have everybody arrive on time for meetings, not only do you have to be ready to start the meeting on time, but you must actually start the meeting on time – regardless of how many people are there when that time arrives. If others in your group arrive a couple of minutes late and the meeting has already started – they are more likely to arrive on time to the next meeting. If, on the other hand, you delayed beginning the meeting until more people arrived, they will continue to be late in the future because they realize, that regardless of what was said about starting on time, you weren't really going to start the meeting until most of the people had arrived.

Another possible goal you may set for yourself in this area of focus could be setting the example of completing the tasks you are assigned. In the same manner as with the previously discussed attribute of punctuality, the people you lead will be very aware of whether or not you follow through with the responsibilities you have been given in your leadership role. As those you lead witness your own level of dedication, they will strive to match that same commitment. Therefore, if you demonstrate a high level of dedication, those around you will also increase their efforts in fulfilling their own responsibilities.

As we conclude this discussion about the importance of the example, take a moment and contemplate the areas of your own life that you can improve upon. Now write down your clear, concise, and specific goals of areas you will improve the life you lead. As you strive to improve your life in these critical areas, others around you will also see your efforts and achievements and want to mimic similar improvements in their own lives.

Remember – don't just lead... ***lead with excellence!***

Power of Example

Long-Range Goal	Deadline
Short-Range Goals	**Deadline**

I have ever deemed it more honorable and more profitable, too, to set a good example than to follow a bad one.

– Thomas Jefferson –

Power of Example

Long-Range Goal	Deadline

Short-Range Goals	Deadline

A good example has twice the value of good advice.
– Anonymous –

Power of Example

Long-Range Goal	Deadline
Short-Range Goals	**Deadline**

Join the ranks of those who live what they teach...
who walk their talk!
– Tony Robbins –

Power of Example

Long-Range Goal	Deadline

Short-Range Goals	Deadline

Nothing is so contagious as example; and we never do any
great good or evil which does not produce its like.
– Francois de la Rochefoucauld –

Chapter 7 – Cooperation in Competition

Chapter 7 – Cooperation in Competition

Leadership is based on inspiration, not domination; on cooperation, not intimidation.
– William Arthur Wood –

Another important aspect of leadership is the ability to get the members of your group to work well together in a spirit of cooperation. Too often, people try to use competition to motivate people to action, but the contention that often accompanies competition can prove to be counterproductive. Through working with high school and junior high school students, I have seen various contests between classes or schools. Some of these have used a spirit of cooperation while others have used a spirit of competition to try to motivate participation. Let me illustrate the differences between the two styles.

One such competition that I remember was an effort to collect canned food for a local food pantry. In an effort to encourage higher levels of participation, the school administration promised a pizza party to the homeroom that collected the most canned food items. While this did motivate some students to bring in canned food items, it did not encourage good feelings throughout the school. I saw students taking canned items from other rooms to take to their own homeroom while others would taunt students in different homerooms. After a few days of the competition, students realized that two or three homerooms were leading the contest by such a margin that all other students would give up trying. After this realization spread throughout the school, very few students continued to bring in canned food items.

Contrast this competitive spirit with a similar event using a more cooperative motivation. A couple of years ago, students from three schools in the area where I live realized a dire need for warm clothing in the far-off land of Mongolia. The student leaders of the three schools decided to see how much clothing the students from the three schools could collectively gather over a two-week period. The result was a unifying project between the three schools that collected 18 semi-trailers full of warm clothing to send to needy people in Mongolia. The three schools involved never did disclose which students brought the most clothes, they simply announced the final joint results. The students from these three schools, rather than harboring ill feelings toward each other as a result of competition, experienced a unifying bond developed through the spirit of cooperation. When members of various groups recognize that they are all working for the good of the whole, cooperation will replace the spirit of competition.

I recently attended a conference where one of the presenters invited everyone in attendance to participate in a demonstration to teach about the advantages of cooperation over competition. The presenter divided the participants into two teams of about 12 people each. He then laid two tarps on the floor fairly close together. These tarps were gray on one side and blue on the other and were about five feet square. Each group was assigned a tarp and told that the entire group had to stand on the tarp – a rather tight fit. The goal was to turn the tarp from the blue side to the gray side, but nobody was allowed to step on the carpet.

Both groups initially struggled to turn their own tarp over. After this unsuccessful beginning, somebody pointed out that the instructions didn't indicate this was a race and perhaps we should work together. Somebody else then suggested that we move as many people as possible to one tarp, making it easier to turn the other tarp over. We could then move everyone back over to the tarp that had been turned over and flip the other tarp. The two teams followed the suggestion and successfully completed the task at hand, while simultaneously building a positive spirit of cooperation rather than fostering a spirit of competition.

Please do not misunderstand, competition is not always bad. When a basketball team takes the court, no question about it – their goal is to score more points than their opponents. However, the spirit of competition can be taken to an extreme. We have all seen athletic teams that don't just have the spirit of competition collectively against their opponent, but they also are competing against each other instead of cooperating for the purpose of a common goal.

A prime example of this detrimental style of competition would be the 2003-2004 Los Angeles Lakers. During the off season, the Los Angeles Lakers assembled a team of all-stars that were thought to be unbeatable and guaranteed of a national championship. This team of all-stars did make it to the NBA Championship Series; however, they ended up being defeated quite soundly by the Detroit Pistons. Many of the sports analysts claimed the reason for this breakdown was a lack of teamwork and an over abundance of worrying about personal statistics rather than the team's score.

Even though the nature of competitive sports dictates that only one team is able to win each game, another goal of everyone involved in the game ought to be to play to the best of their abilities. When viewed in this light, both sides of the competition could succeed, even though one team is given credit for the win and the other team is given the loss.

Consider competition in the Olympic sports. I have watched these sporting events and heard the commentators say things like, "She must be so disappointed with receiving the Silver Medal." After hearing those types of comments, I have sat in my home and thought – is it really that disappointing to be the second best in the world at what you have trained to do? I watch these competitions and have the utmost respect for all of the athletes because they have each won numerous contests just in order to qualify for participation at the world-wide level.

Another arena where the spirit of competition often creates vast amounts of damage is in the world of politics. It seems that every four years as the citizens of the United States prepare to elect a new President, the nation becomes divided through competition rather than united in cooperation. In the 2004 presidential campaign, the candidates from both parties were very accusatory in their debates and characterization of their opponent. However, during an interview with a political commentator, I heard one of the presidential hopefuls candidly admit that both parties held as their primary goal the good of the American citizens, but they just had different ways of accomplishing that goal.

While it is necessary for each candidate and political party to make their views and policies known to the public, these views can be expressed in such a manner as to show respect to everyone involved. By showing a healthy amount of respect for their opponents, the job of bridging the post-election divide would be a much more simple task because the public would have witnessed the genuine respect the candidates have for one another even among their differences.

Applying these principles to the people you are involved with will increase the group's effectiveness in accomplishing any task. Too often individual members of various groups will strive for their personal achievement instead of focusing on the success of the group. As a spirit of cooperation begins to permeate the attitudes of group members, individuals will realize their personal success and accomplishments rely heavily on the ability of the group to accomplish their goals.

Now, as with each chapter in this book, I encourage you to take some time and contemplate what changes you need to make in your life in order to encourage a spirit of cooperation in your various relationships. After you have spent an adequate amount of time pondering about the changes you want to make, write down your goals in a clear, concise, and specific manner. Additionally, do not forget to keep track of the progress you are making in accomplishing these newly established goals as well as all of the goals you have set in the past.

Remember – don't just lead... ***lead with excellence!***

Cooperation vs. Competition

Long-Range Goal	Deadline
Short-Range Goals	**Deadline**

Only justice, fairness, consideration and cooperation can finally lead men to the dawn of eternal peace.
– Dwight D. Eisenhower –

Cooperation vs. Competition

Long-Range Goal	Deadline
Short-Range Goals	**Deadline**

Power consists in one's capacity to link his will with the purpose of others, to lead by reason and a gift of cooperation.
– Woodrow Wilson –

Cooperation vs. Competition

Long-Range Goal	Deadline
Short-Range Goals	**Deadline**

Every kind of peaceful cooperation among men is
primarily based on mutual trust..
– Albert Einstein –

Cooperation vs. Competition

Long-Range Goal	Deadline

Short-Range Goals	Deadline

The only thing that will redeem mankind is cooperation.
– Bertrand Russell –

Chapter 8 – Fan the Flame

Chapter 8 – Fan the Flame

The key to realizing a dream is to focus not on success but on significance - and then even the small steps and little victories along your path will take on greater meaning.
– Oprah Winfrey –

I imagine as I am writing this book that, most likely, all of you reading this book have been camping or at least sat around a campfire before. This chapter will use the example of a campfire for discussing the final leadership skill in this volume.

Think of the last time you built a campfire. You first gathered some kindling – little scraps of wood, pine needles, dry leaves, and other material that would be quick to ignite to get your fire started. Your excitement level at this point of the campfire process was most likely fairly high. You then placed this kindling on the top of some crumpled newspapers that you brought from home. Then you gathered pieces of wood that were slightly larger – twigs, branches, maybe you even used a hatchet to split a larger log. You arranged these next pieces of wood around your kindling, maybe in a teepee or log cabin formation as you learned in your scouting days or girls' camp days. You also have prepared even larger pieces of wood and placed them close enough to the fire to be readily accessible, but far enough away that they won't catch on fire before you place them in the fire pit.

You then strike the match or lighter and ignite the paper. Seeing the flames begin to burn not only warms your body, but also warms your spirit with the excitement of being in the outdoors. In no time at all, the kindling has caught fire and the newspaper has become ash. In turn, this kindling then starts the slightly larger pieces of wood and the fire is crackling nicely. When you notice that the branches and twigs are burning well on their own and the kindling is almost gone, you add two or three of your larger logs to maintain the longevity of the fire. You then sit back, relax and enjoy the warmth and smell of the fire with your family or friends.

Hopefully you have the image of a campfire burning brightly in your mind's eye. But what happens next with this campfire is what I want to focus on and then relate to leadership. As you and your family and friends are enjoying yourselves around the fire, although the coals are glowing a brilliant red, you begin to notice the flames are dying down and you feel a distinct chill in the autumn air.

Almost instinctively, you step toward the fire, pick up two or three of the logs you had prepared earlier and place them on the bed of burning coals. Shortly after returning to your seat, your family and friends begin commenting on the increased amount of smoke coming from the fire and you notice that the newly placed wood has not ignited yet, but is just producing a lot of smoke. So, you rise again from your chair, approach the fire, and kneel down in the dirt next to the fire pit. You bend over and begin blowing at the base of the fire – on what appears to be the hottest of the red coals. After about five or six really strong blows, the flames are leaping into the air again and you are sure the new wood will ignite and burn quite nicely. You rise from the side of the fire, brush the dirt from your knees, and return to your chair feeling slightly lightheaded from the intense blowing.

The first lesson gained from this analogy is illustrated by the blazing flames of the fire slowing diminishing to a mere flicker. I have seen groups and individuals set out with the best of intentions to accomplish a significant goal, only to have their efforts slowly weaken and the participants become discouraged. The discouragement is not a result of a poorly selected goal or as a result of a lack of abilities or talents. This discouragement sets in because the group members have not taken adequate time to rekindle their excitement in achieving the established goal.

In planning everything that must take place in order to accomplish a task, set aside some time for the members of the group to collectively and individually find a renewal of commitment and energy. This time should be separate from and in addition to the time required to accomplish the goal. This time will be well spent as the group renews their excitement to achieve the goal. Just as the fire died from a lack of fresh fuel caused by the consumption of the wood you originally placed during the fire building stage, the desire to achieve a significant goal needs to be constantly nourished. Nobody plans on losing the excitement of achieving a goal, it is a natural process that happens gradually – almost imperceptibly.

This slow process is likened to the proverbial example of how to cook a frog. If you were to place a frog in a pot of boiling water, it would notice the rapid change in temperature and leap from the pot. However, when a frog is placed in a pot of room temperature water and the water is then gradually brought to a boil, the frog will be oblivious to the change in temperature and will simply remain in the pot and be cooked. You must be acutely aware of the attitudes of group members in order to notice the signs of burnout and then work to alleviate the accompanying results.

As a leader, it is vital for you to recognize the signs of burnout within yourself and also within members of your group and then appropriately deal with the issue. An effective way to provide consistent rekindling of the excitement in achieving a goal is to give plenty of public praise and recognition as members of the group accomplish the short-term goals necessary in accomplishing the long-term goals. As members of the group witness other group members receiving accolades and awards, they will become motivated to work harder to receive similar recognition themselves.

Another method for providing renewal from burnout is by taking a break from working on the goal to refocus the efforts of the group. I recall when I was a youth and participating with a Boy Scout troop, we would take retreats on a regular basis for evaluating the progress of the troop and also plan for the future. Growing up in Colorado made it very convenient to get away to the Rocky Mountains for either a day or overnight retreat. These retreats were valuable in determining what activities we would pursue in the future, which merit badges we needed to work on as a troop, and also evaluate the progress we had made since our last retreat.

A second lesson learned from the analogy of the campfire deals with the adding of new wood. The groups you work with are most likely in a state of change all the time. Sometimes group members dropout of the group and, hopefully, new people will be joining your group to contribute to the success of the whole. The analogy of the campfire teaches us what we must do when we have new members join our groups.

When the flames of the campfire were waning, the natural and appropriate response was to place more wood on the fire. However, simply placing the wood on the bed of coals was not enough as that immediately produced an annoying increase of smoke. In order for the newly placed wood to catch fire themselves, it requires somebody else fanning the flame enough to spread the fire to the newly placed wood. As new members join your group, they may require the same type of intense focus until they have caught the spirit of the group goals and vision themselves.

When new members join the group, it is often a good idea to pair them up with another member of the group that is full of enthusiasm in a mentor-type relationship. This enthusiasm can be very contagious and help to get the new members of the group excited about contributing their efforts in accomplishing the goals of the group.

As mentioned earlier, I worked for two years as a missionary in Taiwan. Every four to five weeks new volunteers would arrive. In order to help these newcomers get established in the work and become acquainted with their new environment, they were generally paired with another volunteer who had been in Taiwan for a year or more. This pairing not only allowed the new members of the group to become familiar with the people and culture of Taiwan, but they would also receive training in the goals and purposes promoted throughout the mission. An additional benefit of these companionships was that the fresh zeal and excitement of the newcomer would often serve to rejuvenate their partner also.

As important as this rejuvenation and renewal is for a group, it is equally important on an individual basis. An old axiom states, "All work and no play make Jack a dull boy." Each of us must take time away from the work we perform everyday to relax and find personal rejuvenation. Many people find this renewal through physical activities, such as, sports or other forms of exercise. This can also be achieved by taking time to read a book, play a game, take a walk, personal meditation, or any number of other activities. The purpose of these renewal activities is to break up the monotony of your daily work and allow you to the return to your work with a fresh resolve to accomplish the task at hand.

People who participate in the sport of archery understand this concept in a unique way. When an archer is not going to use their bow for an extended period of time they will loosen the string of their bow. This allows the bow to extend to a greater length and, therefore, work with greater power in the future. If an archer does not loosen the string of their bow, the bow will be accustomed to the stressed position and not have as much spring or power when releasing the arrows.

Our own lives are much the same, if we keep ourselves under constant pressure, we will become tired and worn out. However, if we will take opportunities for renewal, we will then return to our duties with new fervor and excitement for accomplishing the goals at hand.

I previously shared a few suggestions for ways to find personal renewal, but the number of different ways to find renewal are as unique and numerous as people in the world. Explore various methods of personal renewal and find many different avenues for yourself to take. These opportunities for renewal do not have to take a long time or be complex in nature. The key is to make sure the activity provides the relief you need to function at your optimal level of performance.

As we come to the end of this chapter and the end of this book, take one more opportunity to reflect on your own life and areas you may need to improve. After taking a sufficient amount of time to ponder this area of focus, write down your clear, concise, and specific goals. As you work on these goals, remember to track your path to success and find someone you can be accountable to for the progress you make.

Remember – don't just lead... ***lead with excellence!***

Fan the Flame

Long-Range Goal	Deadline

Short-Range Goals	Deadline

When your desires are strong enough, you will appear to possess superhuman powers to achieve.
– Napoleon Hill –

Fan the Flame

Long-Range Goal	Deadline

Short-Range Goals	Deadline

We may be very busy, we may be very efficient, but we will also be truly effective when we begin with the end in mind.
– Stephen R. Covey –

Fan the Flame

Long-Range Goal	Deadline

Short-Range Goals	Deadline

Most of the important things in the world have been accomplished by people who have kept on trying when there seemed to be no hope at all.

– Dale Carnegie –

Fan the Flame

Long-Range Goal	Deadline
Short-Range Goals	**Deadline**

If you want to build a ship, don't herd people together to collect wood and don't assign them tasks and work, but rather teach them to long for the endless immensity of the sea.

– Antoine de Saint-Exupery –

Epilogue

Epilogue

Now that you have reached the end of this book, let me first commend you for your efforts in improving your leadership skills. As you continue to strive to achieve the goals you have set in conjunction with each of the attributes we have discussed, you will notice increased effectiveness in your leadership roles and all aspects of you life.

Although this is the end of this volume, do not let this be the end of your striving for excellence in your leadership and your life. You have learned important principles and how to implement them in your life. As you continue to implement these principles you have learned, you will continue to reap the rewards of your efforts and others around you will notice your efforts also.

As you complete the long-term goals you have established for each chapter while reading this book, set new goals and strive for continual improvement. Remember to write down your goals, review them frequently, and review your progress on a continual basis.

Additional ways to aide in pursuing this continual self-improvement is to look for volume two of *Excellence in Leadership* and learn how to refine 8 more skills to help you develop yourself into a more effective leader and visit my website for leadership tips and news.

www.excellenceinleadershiponline.com

Remember – don't just lead... **lead with excellence!**

References

Hinckley, G. B. (2002). *Way to be!* New York: Simon & Schuster.

Monson, T. S. (1970). *LDS general conference report: October 1970.* Salt Lake City, UT: Deseret Publishing.

About the Author

Dr. Kelly Preston Anderson lives with his wife and three daughters. His work involves teaching high-school and college age students. He also travels as a motivational speaker in conjunction with conferences sponsored by Brigham Young University.

Dr. Anderson holds a bachelor's degree in Mandarin Chinese, a master's degree in education, and a doctorate degree in management and organizational leadership. His personal claim to fame is scoring a perfect 800 on the analytical section of the Graduate Record Examination.

Dr. Anderson spends many hours each week working with church and community groups. In his spare time, Dr. Anderson enjoys spending time with his family, working in his garden and working on his computer.